PASS YOU

KS3 MATHS
Number

Dear Student,

This book has been specially devised to help you prepare for your KS3 National Test by reminding you of the key facts you will need to have at your fingertips when it comes to the actual test. Some aspects of the work in this book you might find easy but it's still important to spend time on these as they will help you to become faster and more efficient.

The KS3 Maths Tests are normally taken in May when you are in Year 9. Your teacher will decide which level of test you should take. Your tests will be at one of the following levels: 3-5 or 4-6 or 5-7 or 6-8. This book is designed especially to help students who are working on levels 4-6 or 5-7, but will also be useful for students working at levels 3-5 or 6-8.

You will sit three tests:

✓ calculator paper,   ✓ non-calculator paper,   ✓ timed mental maths test.

Most of the double page spreads in this book follow the same structure and consist of three sections: 'What You Need to Know', 'Revision Facts' and 'Questions'. Read 'What You Need to Know' carefully, making sure that it makes sense to you. You may find it helpful to work with a friend so that you can check with each other that you both understand. Use the 'Revision Facts' as a reminder - you may like to copy these into an exercise book to create your own personal revision guide to use nearer the test. Try all the 'Questions', even those that are easy but especially those that appear to be difficult.

There is an answer section in the middle of this book that you can pull out to check your work. If you find that you have made a mistake, don't worry but just try to see where you went wrong. You can learn a lot from your mistakes!

To answer some of the questions you will need a calculator.

Good luck,

Andrew Brodie

WHAT YOU NEED TO KNOW

You already know how to add numbers together but it is possible to make errors, particularly when dealing with very large numbers or with several numbers at a time or with numbers that include decimals.

Look at the following examples.

Example 1: 324193 + 49899

Tips:
  i) Identify which digits are the units and line them up.
  ii) Work very neatly, keeping all the digits in line.
  iii) Write the 'carrying digits' very small.
  iv) Look to see if the answer is reasonable.

$$
\begin{array}{r}
324193 \\
+\quad 49899 \\
\hline
374092 \\
\hline
{\scriptstyle 1\ 1\ 1\ 1}
\end{array}
$$

This 3 and this 9 are the units. They are in line and so are all the other digits.

Does the answer seem reasonable?

Because the 3 units add the 9 units make 12, we leave the 2 in the units answer and 'carry' the 1 to the tens. We write the 'carrying digits' very small but they are important.

Example 2: 7214 + 312 + 14957 + 88

$$
\begin{array}{r}
7214 \\
312 \\
14957 \\
+\quad 88 \\
\hline
22571 \\
\hline
{\scriptstyle 1\ 1\ 1\ 2}
\end{array}
$$

Add the units first.

Tips:
  i) Estimate the answer first, by noticing that the biggest number is about 15000 and the next biggest is about 7000 and the others are relatively small so you would expect an answer of about 22000.
  ii) Line up the units, then keep all the other digits in line.
  iii) Work neatly.

Example 3:

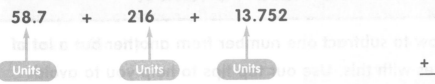

58.7   +   216   +   13.752

Units   Units   Units

Tips:
i) Identify the units.
ii) Write the question neatly in columns.
iii) Show the decimal point for the 216, then fill all the gaps after the decimal points with zeros.
iv) Is the answer reasonable?

```
   58.7
   216
+  13.752
_____


   58.700
  216.000
+  13.752
_____
  288.452
```

REVISION FACT

✓ Always keep the units in line.

QUESTIONS

1   7692417 + 59284

+ _____

_____

2   7416 + 29 + 892 + 764 + 2118

+ _____

_____

3   19 + 5.82 + 69.7

+ _____

_____

WHAT YOU NEED TO KNOW

b) Long division

Compare short division to long division: 370 ÷ 5

Both methods give the same answer to the same question.

$$5{\overline{)37^20}} \quad 74$$

$$\begin{array}{r} 74 \\ 5{\overline{)370}} \\ -35 \\ \hline 20 \\ -20 \\ \hline 0 \end{array}$$

We simply subtract the 35 here.

Then bring down the zero to make 20.

We can subtract 20 because 4 x 5 = 20.

Here are some more examples:

Example 1: 348 ÷ 12 by long division:

$$\begin{array}{r} 2 \\ 12{\overline{)348}} \\ -24 \\ \hline 10 \end{array}$$

Because 2 x 12 = 24.

Bring down the 8 to make 108.

$$\begin{array}{r} 29 \\ 12{\overline{)348}} \\ -24 \\ \hline 108 \\ -108 \\ \hline 0 \end{array}$$

Because 9 x 12 = 108.

Look how similar this example is.

Example 2: 345 ÷ 12

$$\begin{array}{r} 28 \\ 12{\overline{)345.00}} \\ -24 \\ \hline 105 \\ -96 \\ \hline 9 \end{array}$$

105 is not big enough to give us 9 twelves.

We need to put a decimal point and some zeros.

$$\begin{array}{r} 28.75 \\ 12{\overline{)345.00}} \\ -24 \\ \hline 105 \\ -96 \\ \hline 90 \\ -84 \\ \hline 60 \\ -60 \\ \hline 0 \end{array}$$

2 x 12

8 x 12

7 x 12

5 x 12

REVISI

✓ When
numbe

Tips:

i) Long division is exactly the same process as short division but can be easier because you have space to subtract.

ii) Keep subtracting what you have used then bring the next number down.

iii) Work very tidily so that you bring the correct number down each time.

iv) Some questions will go on for ever – you need to decide when to stop.

QUEST

1 9 ÷ 1.5

3 38 ÷ 1.

5 27 ÷ 1.2

QUESTIONS

1 $13\overline{)351}$

2 $17\overline{)663}$

Tip: You may need to try multiplying 17 by different numbers less than 10 to see how many you use at each stage.

3 $23\overline{)618}$

4 $14\overline{)892}$

WHAT YOU NEED TO KNOW

$1 \times 1 = 1$

$1^2 = 1$

$2 \times 2 = 4$

$2^2 = 4$

$3 \times 3 = 9$

$3^2 = 9$

$4 \times 4 = 16$

$4^2 = 16$

Tip: You need to know all square numbers up to 10^2

REVISION FACT

✓ A square number is the result of a number being multiplied by itself.

QUESTIONS

1 $5^2 = $ ....

2 $9^2 = $ ....

3 $6^2 = $ ....

4 $10^2 = $ ....

5 $7^2 = $ ....

6 $11^2 = $ ....

7 $8^2 = $ ....

8 $12^2 = $ ....

For the next questions you could use long multiplication or you could use your calculator. Here is an example: 17^2. On the calculator, press the following keys: **1** **7** **x^2** **=**

You should get the answer 289

9 $13^2 = $ ....

10 $14^2 = $ ....

11 $15^2 = $ ....

12 $20^2 = $ ....

13 $25^2 = $ ....

14 $30^2 = $ ....

15 $3.2^2 = $ ....

16 $6.9^2 = $ ....

17 $12.6^2 = $ ....

ANSWERS

p3

1
```
  7692417
+   59284
  ───────
  7751701
  ¹¹¹¹¹
```

> Notice how the digits are kept in line. This helps to avoid serious errors.

2
```
  7416
    29
   892
   764
+ 2118
  ─────
 11219
  ² ² ²
```

> Always use tiny carrying figures.

3
```
  19.00
   5.82
+ 69.70
  ─────
  94.52
   ² ¹
```

> Don't forget the decimal point in the answer.

p5

1
```
  ²¹⁷8.0
-  89.6
  ─────
 128.4
```

2
```
  6⁶⁹¹00
- 1214
  ─────
 5486
```

3
```
  2⁶⁹7.00
-  3.45
  ─────
 23.55
```

4
```
 1⁵⁸⁹⁹⁹0000.0
-    4987.3
  ─────────
 11012.7
```

p7

1
```
        78
    x   23
        ───
 78 x 3 → 234
           ₂
 78 x 20→ 1560
           ₁
        ────
        1794
```

2
```
     516
   x   7
     ───
   3612
    ₁ ₄
```

3
```
      842
    x  30
    ─────
    25260
      ₁
```

> Put a zero in the units because you are multiplying by tens.

4
```
     294
   x  36
   ─────
    1764
     ₅ ₂
    8820
     ₂ ₁
   ─────
   10584
      ₁
```

5
```
     627
   x  19
   ─────
    5643
     ₂ ₆
    6270
   ─────
   11913
      ₁
```

6
```
      25
    x 25
    ────
     125
      ₂
     500
      ₁
    ────
     625
```

7 $3.9 \times 1.3 =$
```
      39
   x  13
   ────
    117
    390
   ────
    507   so 3.9 x 1.3 = 5.07
```

8 $7.82 \times 2.4 =$
```
      782
   x   24
   ─────
    3128
   15640
   ─────
   18768   so 7.82 x 2.4 = 18.768
```

WHAT YOU NEED TO KNOW

This is an index number.

... so is this

$2^2 = 4$

$2^3 = 8$

Tip: Index numbers are sometimes called 'indices'. The word 'indices' is the plural of 'index'.

Look:

We say 'two to the power four'.

We say 'two to the power four is sixteen'.

$2^4 = 2 \times 2 \times 2 \times 2 = 16$

The index number shows us how many times the number is multiplying itself.

$3^5 = 3 \times 3 \times 3 \times 3 \times 3 = 243$

This is the index number.

To use the calculator to find the same answer press: 3 x^y 5 =

Note: some calculators have this key instead: y^x

REVISION FACTS

✓ The index number shows the number of times a number is multiplying itself.

✓ To find a power using your calculator press x^y

QUESTIONS

1 $6^4 = $ _____

2 $7^5 = $ _____

3 $2^9 = $ _____

4 $3^7 = $ _____

5 $10^4 = $ _____

6 $8^6 = $ _____

7 $2^{18} = $ _____

WHAT YOU NEED TO KNOW

Look:

$$2^3 \quad \times \quad 2^2 = 32$$
$$(2 \times 2 \times 2) \times (2 \times 2) = 32$$
$$2^5 = 32$$

So, when a number with an index number is multiplied by the same number with an index number you can add the indices.

Look at another example: $3^5 \times 3^2 = 3^7$

Now use the calculator: $\boxed{3}\ \boxed{x^y}\ \boxed{7}\ \boxed{=}$
to find the answer: 2187

REVISION FACT

✓ $x^3 \times x^2 = x^5$ **Just add the indices**

QUESTIONS

Simplify the following then use your calculator to find the answer. The first one has been started for you.

1 $2^4 \times 2^2 = \underline{2^6} = \underline{\hspace{3cm}}$

2 $6^2 \times 6^3 = \underline{\hspace{1.5cm}} = \underline{\hspace{3cm}}$

3 $3^3 \times 3^9 = \underline{\hspace{1.5cm}} = \underline{\hspace{3cm}}$

4 $10^3 \times 10 = \underline{\hspace{1.5cm}} = \underline{\hspace{3cm}}$

Tip: This means 10^1

'ten to the power one' is 10.

QUESTIONS

Use your calculator to find the answers to these questions:

1 $2^0 = $ ....

2 $6^0 = $ ....

3 $10^0 = $ ....

4 $26^0 = $ ....

Do you remember how to enter it: 2 x^n 0 =

Note: This is a zero, not a degrees sign!

WHAT YOU NEED TO KNOW

You should have found that all of the questions above produced the same answer.

Tip: You can see that any number to the power zero equals 1.

The next set of questions will show you another important rule.

QUESTIONS

5 $3^7 = $ ....

6 $3^2 = $ ....

Use your answers to (5) and (6) for question **7** $3^7 \div 3^2 = $ ....

Now find the answer to question **8** $3^5 = $ ....

WHAT YOU NEED TO KNOW

You should have found that your answer to question (8) was the same as your answer to question (7). This shows that $3^7 \div 3^2 = 3^5$

We have simply subtracted the indices: 7 – 2 = 5

REVISION FACTS

✓ $x^0 = 1$ Any number to the power zero = 1

✓ $x^5 \div x^2 = x^3$ Just subtract the indices.

QUESTIONS

Simplify the following, then use your calculator to find the answer. The first one has been started for you.

1 $2^8 \div 2^5 =$ ...2^3... = ...

2 $4^9 \div 4^7 =$ ...... = ...

3 $6^7 \div 6 =$ ...... = ...

4 $3^6 \div 3^6 =$ ...... = ...

Tip: Don't forget, if no index number is shown, this means 6^1.

The next questions will give you some revision but will also show you something new. Use your calculator to show all the values.

5
$2^{10} =$ ....

$2^9 =$ ....

$2^8 =$ ....

$2^7 =$ ....

$2^6 =$ ....

$2^5 =$ ....

$2^4 =$ ....

$2^3 =$ ....

$2^2 =$ ....

$2^1 =$ ....

$2^0 =$ ....

$2^{-1} =$ ....

$2^{-2} =$ ....

Each rung on the ladder is the one above divided by 2.

This is worth $\frac{1}{2}$

This is worth $\frac{1}{4}$

$\frac{1}{4}$ is the same as $\frac{1}{2^2}$

6
$3^{10} =$ ....

$3^9 =$ ....

$3^8 =$ ....

$3^7 =$ ....

$3^6 =$ ....

$3^5 =$ ....

$3^4 =$ ....

$3^3 =$ ....

$3^2 =$ ....

$3^1 =$ ....

$3^0 =$ ....

$3^{-1} =$ ....

$3^{-2} =$ ....

Tip: These two will need to be shown as recurring decimals.
eg. 0.33333... can be written 0.3̇

the dot shows it's recurring.

WHAT YOU NEED TO KNOW

Look at how we can make these two numbers by multiplying integers.

> Tip: Did you know that 'integer' is just a fancy name for a whole number?

144		149	
1 x 144		1 x 149	
144 x 1		149 x 1	
12 x 12			
6 x 24			
24 x 6			
3 x 48			
48 x 3			
8 x 18			
18 x 8			
4 x 36			
36 x 4			
2 x 72			
72 x 2			
16 x 9			
9 x 16			

This is an impressive list ...

... but this isn't, because 149 is a prime number

> Tip: When a number only has itself and 1 as its factors, it is called a prime number.

Each column shows a list of the factors of 144. In order of size, the factors of 144 are: 1, 2, 3, 4, 6, 8, 9, 12, 16, 18, 24, 36, 48, 72, 144
The factors of 149 are: 1, 149

REVISION FACTS

✓ Factors of a number are integers which multiply together to make that number.

✓ Prime numbers have only two factors; themselves and 1.

QUESTIONS

List all the factors for each of the numbers below. Draw a ring around each of the prime numbers.

1 18 ☐ ☐ ☐ ☐ ☐ ☐

2 16 ☐ ☐ ☐ ☐ ☐

3 2 ☐ ☐

4 12 ☐ ☐ ☐ ☐ ☐ ☐

5 7 ☐ ☐

6 20 ☐ ☐ ☐ ☐ ☐ ☐

7 3 ☐ ☐

8 5 ☐ ☐

9 13 ☐ ☐

10 10 ☐ ☐ ☐ ☐

11 11 ☐

12 24 ☐ ☐ ☐ ☐ ☐ ☐ ☐ ☐

13 36 ☐ ☐ ☐ ☐ ☐ ☐ ☐ ☐ ☐

14 17 ☐ ☐

Look at the numbers above to help you with these questions.

15 What is the **only** even prime number? ☐

16 What are the common factors of 24 and 36? 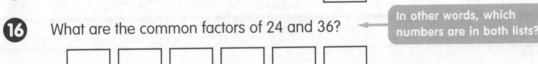 *In other words, which numbers are in both lists?*

☐ ☐ ☐ ☐ ☐ ☐

17 What is the highest common factor of 24 and 36? ☐

18 What is the highest common factor of 12 and 20? ☐

WHAT YOU NEED TO KNOW

Look:

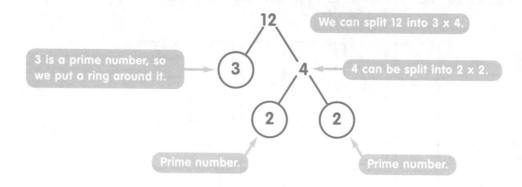

3 is a prime number, so we put a ring around it.

We can split 12 into 3 x 4.

4 can be split into 2 x 2.

Prime number.

Prime number.

So we can see that 12 = 2 x 2 x 3

or 12 = 2^2 x 3

Tip: This is called 'expressing 12 as a product of its prime factors'.

Here is another example. You can see that there is more than one way to split it.

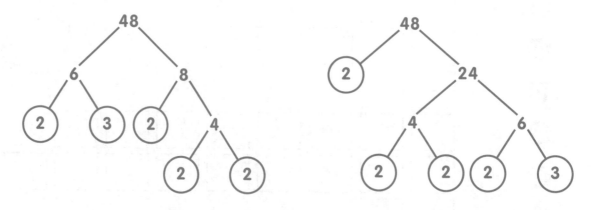

In both cases you can see that 48 = 2 x 2 x 2 x 2 x 3

= 2^4 x 3

REVISION FACTS

✓ Express a number as a product of its prime factors by splitting the number and drawing rings around the prime numbers you find.

✓ Write the prime factors in order. eg. 2^2 x 3 x 5 <u>not</u> 5 x 3 x 2^2

QUESTION

Express the following numbers as products of their prime factors.

1   36   **2**   45

3   84   **4**   96

WHAT YOU NEED TO KNOW

We can find the highest common factor (HCF) of two numbers by expressing the numbers as products of their prime factors, then seeing which factors appear in both.

For example $84 = 2^2 \times 3 \times 7$ and $96 = 2^5 \times 3$

Don't forget that $2^5 = 2^2 \times 2^3$

The factors in both are 2^2 and 3...

... so the HCF of 84 and 96 = $2^2 \times 3 = 12$

QUESTION

5 What is the HCF of 36 and 45?

WHAT YOU NEED TO KNOW

Look at the number line.

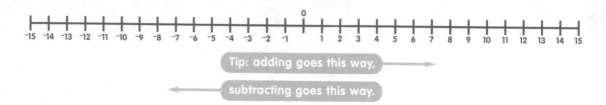

Tip: adding goes this way,

subtracting goes this way.

Look at the following examples.

Example 1: $^-3 + 4$

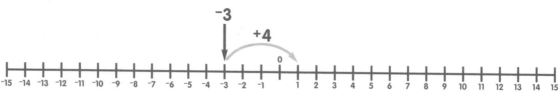

...so $^-3 + 4 = 1$ (negative 3 plus 4 = 1)

Example 2: $^-3 - 4$

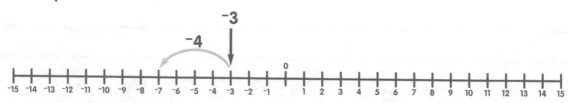

...so $^-3 - 4 = ^-7$ (negative 3 minus 4 = negative 7)

But look carefully at this example.

$^-3 - ^-4$

Tip: Two minuses <u>together</u> make a plus.

...so $^-3 - ^-4 = ^-3 + 4 = 1$ (negative 3 minus negative 4 = 1)

Compare these two examples:

$^-2 - 6 = ^-8$ $2 - ^-6 = 8$

REVISION FACTS

✓ On a number line we can see that

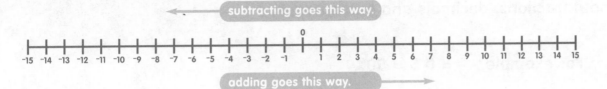

subtracting goes this way.

adding goes this way.

✓ Where two negative signs are **together** you get a plus.
'Two minuses make a plus', eg. $-\ ^-5 = +5$

QUESTIONS

1 $2 - 4 =$ ....

2 $2 - \ ^-4 =$ ....

3 $5 - 6 =$ ....

4 $1 - 7 =$ ....

5 $6 - \ ^-3 =$ ....

6 $^-2 - 3 =$ ....

7 $^-4 + 5 =$ ....

8 $^-4 - \ ^-4 =$ ....

9 $^-1 - \ ^-6 =$ ....

10 The temperature in London at noon is 8°C. The temperature in Vancouver at noon is ⁻4°C.

a) What is the difference in temperatures?

....

b) At midnight, the temperature in London has gone down by 6°C.
What is the new temperature in London?

....

c) At midnight, the temperature in Vancouver has gone down by 10°C.
What is the new temperature in Vancouver?

....

d) What is the difference in temperatures between the two cities
at midnight?

....

WHAT YOU NEED TO KNOW

This table shows some facts that you should learn. It shows matching facts about fractions, decimals and percentages.

For example, $\frac{1}{2} = 0.5 = 50\%$

Fraction	Decimal	Percentage
$\frac{1}{2}$	0.5	50%
$\frac{1}{4}$	0.25	25%
$\frac{3}{4}$	0.75	75%
$\frac{1}{3}$	$0.\dot{3}$	$33.\dot{3}\%$
$\frac{2}{3}$	$0.\dot{6}$	$66.\dot{6}\%$
$\frac{1}{10}$	0.1	10%
$\frac{1}{5}$	0.2	20%
$\frac{3}{10}$	0.3	30%
$\frac{2}{5}$	0.4	40%
$\frac{3}{5}$	0.6	60%
$\frac{7}{10}$	0.7	70%
$\frac{4}{5}$	0.8	80%
$\frac{9}{10}$	0.9	90%
$\frac{1}{8}$	0.125	12.5%

$\frac{1}{2}$ is equivalent to $\frac{5}{10}$

Note that $\frac{1}{5}$ is equivalent to $\frac{2}{10}$

is equivalent to $\frac{4}{10}$

is equivalent to $\frac{8}{10}$

Notice the dots to show the recurring digits.

To change a fraction to a decimal, use your calculator to divide the numerator by the denominator.

Look $\frac{3}{8}$ ⟶ top ÷ bottom ⟶ 3 ÷ 8 = 0.375

We can now change this to a percentage by multiplying by 100.

0.375 x 100 = 37.5   so $\frac{3}{8}$ = 0.375 = 37.5%